IMAGES
of England

CHAPELTOWN AND HIGH GREEN

Bonfire at Lady's Folly, Tankersley Park, erected by Newton Chambers as part of the Coronation Day celebrations of King George V on 22 June 1911. The girth at the bottom was 116 feet and it was 35 feet high and contained 185 tons of timber. In the background on the left is Lady's Folly itself, built in the 1760s by the second Marquis of Rockingham for his wife, Mary. It was a summer house/observatory with views to the east over Tankersley Park towards Wentworth. It was demolished in 1960.

IMAGES
of England

CHAPELTOWN AND HIGH GREEN

Compiled by
Joan and Mel Jones
on behalf of
Chapeltown and High Green Archive

TEMPUS

First published 1996
Reprinted 2000

Tempus Publishing Limited
The Mill, Brimscombe Port,
Stroud, Gloucestershire, GL5 2QG

ISBN 0 7524 0652 3

Typesetting and origination by
Tempus Publishing Limited
Printed in Great Britain by
Midway Clark Printing, Wiltshire

You are here! The crossroads (now roundabout) at Chapeltown in the days of gaslighting and light traffic.

Contents

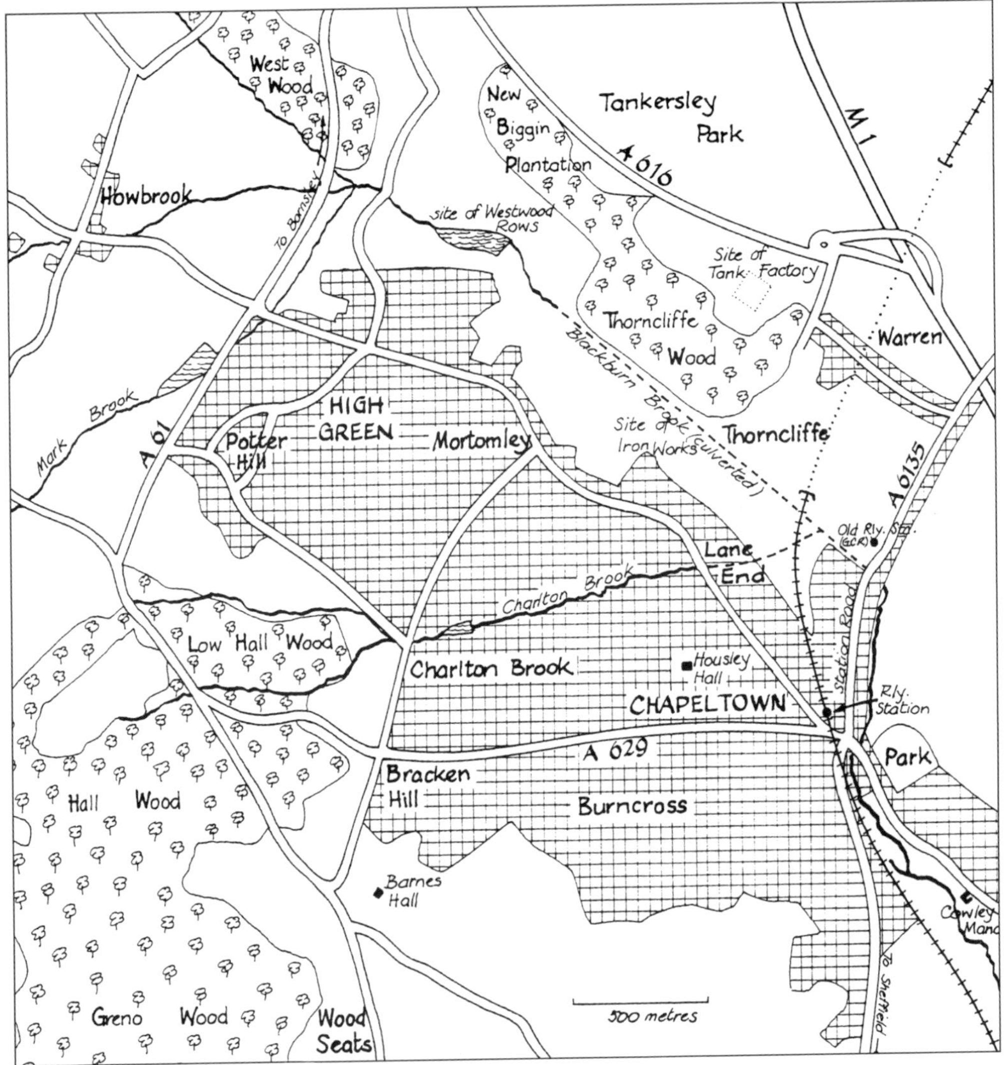

Chapeltown and High Green.

Introduction

Chapeltown and High Green together with a number of smaller settlements – Lane End, Charlton Brook, Mortomley, Burncross, Bracken Hill and Warren – now form a rather shapeless residential suburban fringe on the northern boundary of Sheffield Metropolitan District. Howbrook, which is detached from the other settlements by a tract of agricultural countryside, is a suburbanised village just across the metropolitan district boundary in Barnsley. To the modern visitor these places present nothing out of the ordinary: they are indistinguishable in many respects from thousands of other edge of city residential districts. Yet for a century and a half they were industrial villages that had grown out of their agricultural origins towards the end of the eighteenth century to become, collectively, one of the crucibles of the Industrial Revolution.

Modern industrial development began in the area with the establishment of the so-called Chapel Furnace beside the Blackburn Brook next to White Lane. It was a flourishing concern as early as 1628 and had probably originated sometime in the second half of the previous century. Until about 1780 it was fuelled by charcoal obtained from neighbouring woods. After that date until about 1860 it was coke fuelled and the tenants had associated coal as well as ironstone pits.

However, by the end of the eighteenth century industrial activity at Chapel Furnace was rivalled by developments less than a mile further up the Blackburn valley, developments that were eventually to overshadow and then eclipse it. This was the Thorncliffe Ironworks of Newton Chambers built on land belonging to Earl Fitzwilliam of nearby Wentworth Woodhouse. The first lease from the Earl in December 1793 gave the firm the right to erect blast furnaces and other industrial buildings in the meadows beside the Blackburn Brook and to mine for coal and ironstone in the surrounding countryside. At one time or another the firm operated four collieries in the immediate vicinity of the works. The company mined its own ironstone around the works until about 1880, after which time it was brought by rail from Lincolnshire and Northamptonshire, giving rise to a complex system of branch railways and sidings around the works.

The nineteenth and early twentieth centuries was a period of almost uninterrupted expansion for Newton Chambers including the acquisition of Chapel Furnace. From a labour force of no more than a dozen at Thorncliffe on New Year's Day in 1794 when work began on making the first sough to drain the proposed mine workings, there were about 300 by 1800, and a century later the company employed more than 8,000. At first they manufactured small cast iron goods such as anvils, bedsteads, bootscrapers, irons, pans, pipes, spouts and stoves. Although these light castings continued to be made into the twentieth century, by 1815 the company was also producing heavy castings including beams, forge hammers and rails for waggon roads. At about the same time the firm began to manufacture gas lighting plant and later gasworks plant. Gasworks plant was manufactured in the nineteenth century for hundreds of towns and cities at home and abroad including a complete plant in 1888 for Buenos Aires that was supplied with Thorncliffe coal until the outbreak of the First World War.

By-products of the preparation of coke for the blast furnaces at Thorncliffe were gases, tars and oils. By the beginning of the 1890s, a germicidal disinfectant had been developed from the oils and in 1893 it was patented as Izal. Before the end of the century it was available in liquid, soap, powder, cream and ointment forms. In the early 1900s the firm began a world-wide campaign to get Izal products noticed and adopted by Government departments and medical authorities. Within a few years agencies to market Izal products had been established in countries as far apart as South Africa, Egypt, Canada and India.

Another significant step in the diversification of the company was the agreement reached in 1935 to manufacture excavators under licence from the American firm of Paulin and Harnischfeger. In 1938 the erection of a new excavator plant was begun but before it was completed the Second World War began and it was converted into a tank factory where 1,160 Churchill tanks were produced by the end of the war. After the war, excavator production was resumed, from the late 1940s under licence from the Milwaukee firm of Koehring, the machines going under the name of NCK. In 1958 Newton Chambers bought out Ransome and Rapiers of Ipswich, effectively doubling the firm's excavator production capacity.

After trading independently for over 180 years, Newton Chambers were taken over by Central & Sheerwood in 1973, subsequently completely re-organised, and the most valuable part (the Chemical Division including the Izal factory) sold off. Much of the Thorncliffe site has now been developed as a modern industrial estate and the former collieries and coking plants in the surrounding district have disappeared.

Despite the existence of other local employers and the loss of the collieries through Nationalisation in 1947, during its existence Newton Chambers & Co. had an all pervading influence on the local economy and landscape and on important aspects of local leisure and culture. This is reflected in the selection of photographs in this collection. Outside the section specifically devoted to the firm, its presence is obvious – in the people it attracted to the area and employed, in the retail and other businesses that it indirectly sustained and the cultural and sporting activities that it supported.

This collection of photographs, spanning more than a century, forms part of the extensive collection of photographs, films, documents, artefacts and oral evidence called the Chapeltown and High Green Archive, which is an ever-expanding depository of local historical material safeguarded and managed by a group of local enthusiasts who also publish a wide variety of local history books and booklets based on the Archive's collection. The images in this collection have been carefully selected to provide a comprehensive pictorial record of a highly significant period in the economic and social history of the area, a period that not only saw the population expand considerably but during which a distinctive character and vibrant culture developed. We hope the volume will be of lasting interest to long-established residents and relative newcomers alike.

One

Setting the Scene

This section takes the reader on a preliminary photographic tour of the district. Starting at the centre of Chapeltown the reader is transported along Station Road before returning and travelling along Burncross Road through Greenside to Burncross and Charlton Brook. Lane End and Thorncliffe are investigated and then the tour takes the reader on to Mortomley and High Green. The final leg of the tour crosses the Blackburn Brook to Westwood and Warren. The photographs in this section were all taken when the individual settlements had their own identity, before coalescing into one continuous built-up area.

Gibson's store at Chapeltown. This is probably the oldest photograph in our collection. It was taken in the early Victorian period, possibly in the 1850s or 1860s. The store stood at the junction of the present Station Road and Cowley Lane (see map). The shop had originally been the 'truck' shop for Newton Chambers and managed by Thomas Chambers, the son of one of the firm's founders. Workmen were paid part of their wages in the form of tickets or tokens that could only be exchanged for goods at the firm's shop. Truck shops were abolished by the Truck Act of 1831 which stipulated that workpeople should only be paid in cash. In 1845 the store was in the possession of Thomas Chambers and described in White's Directory for that year as 'grocer & draper, Post Office'. By the time the photograph was taken the store had been subdivided into two shops which were in the possession of Thomas and John Gibson, sons of Mary Chambers (daughter of Thomas Chambers) who married the Revd Ralph Gibson. In White's Directory of 1856 the Gibson brothers were described as 'grocers, drapers and druggists'. It appears that John Gibson was the grocer/draper and Thomas Gibson's shop combined the functions of post office and drug store. John Gibson had been apprenticed to a chemist in Guisborough, in the then North Riding, and it not surprising that he should introduce this trade to Chapeltown As late as about 1903 Thomas Gibson's shop was still a chemist's and Chapeltown post office. The building is also shown on the right in the photograph of central Chapeltown on page 12 taken *c.* 1920, when it was still a chemist's and post office.

Chapeltown from the park, looking west. The Midland Railway bridge (built 1891) carrying the line from Sheffield to Barnsley announces that this is Chapeltown home of Newton Chambers. In the background can be seen the spire of St John's church and the tower of Mt. Pleasant Chapel.

Chapeltown from Ecclesfield Road looking north in the 1920s. Beyond Chapeltown Central Garage can be seen the backs of Smith Street. On the extreme right is the Midland Railway. In the background on the left can be seen the spire of St John's church and the tower of Mt. Pleasant Chapel.

The centre of Chapeltown with the old Wagon & Horses hotel. Its location on the main Sheffield to Barnsley road is reflected in the sign indicating that good stabling was to be had there. On the left is Ellis's clothes shop (see page 34).

Another shot of the centre of Chapeltown in the early 1920s. The old Wagon & Horses has been replaced by the new Waggon & Horses. The old truck shop still stands on the opposite side of the road, part of it still occupied by a chemist's. Beyond the chemist's is the Midland Bank building.

Station Road, Chapeltown looking towards White Lane early this century. In the foreground are three young miners returning from work, and behind, the three brass balls of Whitaker's pawn shop. The white-aproned figure is a barber standing at the door of his shop below the barber's pole.

Station Road about 1912 showing the recently built Picture Palace and adverts for its star picture of the week *'Neath the Lion's Paw.*

Chapeltown formerly had two railway stations: the one at the far end of Station Road up White Lane was the Great Central Railway station; the one shown here is the Midland Railway station, which is still operational, but which has been moved further south for easier access to the centre of Chapeltown and to the Asda superstore. Some of the old station buildings still remain.

The Yorkshire Penny Bank, built about 1900, with the bank manager's house above. It was demolished in 1970. Behind, to the left, on Burncross Road, is the Midland Hotel, now the Carousel. Across the road from the Midland Hotel (far left) is Burncross Farm.

Greenside about 1900. The shop belonged to Edward Milns. The front part of the shop was a drapery business. Beyond the drapery shop was a passage which led to a side door into a grocery shop. The former drapery shop is now a fish and chip shop. The local children, who, as usual have followed the photographer, who would have been conspicuous because of all his paraphernalia, appear to be shouting for reinforcements. Everyone is wearing headgear, caps for boys and boaters or woollen berets for girls. Note the state-of-the-art perambulator on the left.

Bath House Farm which was on the south side of Burncross Road where the recently demolished high-rise flats were built. Its name was derived from the fact that it stood on the site of a stream-fed bath house for the nearby Housley Hall. It was last tenanted by Clement Hall.

Looking towards Burncross Road and the solid stone-built Housley Villas. Beyond, from left to right, are Housley Manor (not to be confused with Housley Hall), the tower of Mt. Pleasant Chapel and the spire of St John's church.

Another view of Burncross Road looking towards the centre of Chapeltown.

Burncross post office about 1900. Standing in the doorway is the owner Jim Stringer, who combined the role of postmaster with that of draper, boot and shoe retailer and general dealer. Note the clay pipe smoker on the left and, perhaps, shop assistants on the right.

Smithy Car(r), now demolished, with its cottage garden.

Chapel Road, Burncross, near the junction with Burncross Road, about 1900. The Primitive Methodist Chapel, opened in 1865 has been recently demolished.

Sweet Pea Row, a colourful corner of old Chapeltown which still stands off Chapel Road at Burncross. When this photograph was taken in the early summer in about 1900, the row lived up to its name with every house bedecked with the two-toned pink flowers. It was probably Sunday, with the menfolk at home, the children dressed for chapel and the smell of Yorkshire puddings wafting from the open doorways. The cottages were typical of their type: stone-built with a good sized living room and a small kitchen on the ground floor, and a large and small bedroom above.

Charlton Brook Dam about 1965 looking towards Stanley Road and the cottages in Charlton Brook Foundry yard.

Charlton Brook Farm about 1965, then occupied by the Simpson family who had farmed there for many years. All the farm buildings have since been converted into residences.

Lane End, Chapeltown viewed from Mt. Pleasant Chapel in the early 1900s. On the left in the middle distance beyond the line of washing, the row of houses is Lane End almshouses built sometime after 1693 on the instructions of Edward Sylvester (see page 42).

Lane End Bridge about 1900. On the extreme right is the Bridge Inn which ceased life as a pub in 1956 and was demolished about 1960. In the garden to the left of the Bridge Inn is a beehive in the shape of a doll's house.

Lane End looking towards Mt. Pleasant Chapel about 1900. Note the rut-marked unmade road. The building with the sign to the Barrel Inn was not the Inn itself but a convenient house-end on which to advertise its presence. The pub was to the right. An old inhabitant who lived in the end house has told us that people sometimes came into their front room in search of a pint of Bentley's!

Looking south-east across Charlton Brook from Lane End towards Mt. Pleasant Chapel and St John's church.

Part of Thorncliffe Rows built for Newton Chambers in the 1860s to house blackleg miners during labour disputes. There was a nine months lockout of miners in 1866 and another of seventeen months from March 1869 to August 1870. The latter dispute stemmed from the decision of Newton Chambers to reduce wages by seven per cent and their refusal to negotiate with the Miners' Union. Workers were to continue to be employed provided they agreed to abide by the rules and by-laws of the company's collieries which involved them in, among other things, negotiating individually over wages and working an eight hour day when required to do so. On 24 March 1869, 850 men and boys were locked out, although several hundred remained at work. On 29 April 1869, although there was a police contingent present, Thorncliffe Rows were attacked by about 200 striking miners. An eyewitness who was living in the Thorncliffe Rows at the time said that they smashed all the windows in five of the cottages and caused the police to scatter in all directions, some hiding in the water closets. No one was injured. The cottages were demolished in the late 1960s.

Thorncliffe Lane leading to Thorncliffe Ironworks at the end of the nineteenth century. The houses were built by Newton Chambers for their foremen and overseers. Note the carefully 'donkey stoned' steps and cellar grates and the wall on the right topped by furnace slag, known locally as 'crozzle'.

Thorncliffe Ironworks from the bottom of Thorncliffe Lane in the early 1900s. The works, which were founded in 1793, occupied the valley of the Blackburn Brook which formed the boundary between Ecclesfield and Tankersley parishes. The two blast furnaces on the left were built in 1873-74 and replaced by a mechanised furnace in 1927.

Mortomley Lane, High Green, looking north-west just before its junction with Greengate Lane. Green Gate Lodge is the most distant house shown. Other interesting features include the ton of coal which has been delivered onto the pavement and the rag and bone man with his horse and cart walking away from the camera.

Mortomley Park, High Green. St Saviour's church is just visible on the left, with Thorncliffe Wood in the background.

Mortomley Hill, early this century. On the left is Furness's sweet shop; the other three shopfronts are Bostwick's who were newsagents. Over Bostwick's shop was a billiard saloon and through the darkened entry, sometimes called the 'Marble Arch', was a yard containing old cottages. To the right was a sweet shop, now a post office, and then the market place and fairground. Markets were held here before the First World War and then for a short period afterwards. The area in front of these shops was used for many years as the assembly point for the congregations of the High Green church and chapels with their banners for the annual Whitsuntide sing. They then joined the congregations of the church and chapels of Chapeltown for a combined Sing on the 'Ten Acre' (see page 98).

Looking down Thompson Hill with the Travellers' Inn on the right. This building still stands but is no longer a pub.

Looking up Thompson Hill with the Travellers' Inn behind the photographer. The lane going off to the left is Potter Hill. The field was used as a pound for stray cattle.

Wortley Road (then called Rotherham Road) at the far end of High Green in the early 1920s with the Salutation Inn on the right. Jean Huddlestone in her *Geography of Childhood*, in which she evokes life in Howbrook and High Green in the late 1920s and 1930s, describes graphically how this point in her journey to school in High Green from the hamlet of Howbrook marked the change from a rural to an industrial community, and from a safe to a dangerous world: 'There were two danger points, one just before the Salutation. From a yard there a gang of small, poorly-clad boys would pour out and attack if we happened to be passing as they set off for school. They had close-cropped heads like moles, sockless feet often, in clumsy boots, short trousers below the knee, men's grey flannel trousers, chopped off and too baggy for their thin bodies, often with great rents in them, and raggy jerseys. In a gang, with their threshing arms, kicking feet and shouted abuse, they were formidable.'

One of the two Westwood Rows shortly before their demolition in the late 1960s. Like the Thorncliffe Rows (see page 23) they were at the centre of riots during the lockout of 1869/70. On 21 January 1870 a crowd, variously estimated at between 300 and 1,500 men, armed with pistols, spiked bludgeons and picks, attacked the Rows and overwhelmed the small police garrison. Police reinforcements came from Barnsley and another battle took place. Twenty-three men were sent for trial at York assizes. The area once occupied by the cottages was landscaped by South Yorkshire County Council in the late 1970s.

Westwood Station, on the Blackburn Valley line of the Great Central Railway, built about 1876 and closed in 1940. The final traces of the station disappeared during the landscaping of the Westwood area in 1978.

Warren Lane looking north-west towards Thorncliffe Wood in the late 1940s. In the right foreground, the disturbed ground marks the edge of the opencast coal mining at Hood Hill. In the right background can be seen the still camouflaged Newton Chambers tank factory in which more than 1000 Churchill tanks were manufactured during the Second World War (see pages 83 and 84). In front of the tank factory can be seen the aerial ropeway connecting Thorncliffe Ironworks with Rockingham Colliery.

Two

Landmarks

The Chapeltown and High Green area is surrounded by woods and farmland and, to the north, by Tankersley Park, originally a medieval deer park. These areas of countryside have always been heavily used for recreation by the local population and have a special place in the memories of long-established residents and those who have left the area. The same can be said of the two small streams running through the area – Blackburn Brook and Charlton Brook where fishing and tadpoling did, and still does, take place. Although the industrial landmarks – the blast furnaces, the colliery headgear and the spoil heaps – which once dominated the landscape have now disappeared, the area is still generously endowed with distinctive buildings. These range from historic houses such as Barnes Hall, Cowley Manor and Housley Hall; houses such as Staindrop Lodge and Greenhead House that accommodated local industrial magnates; churches and chapels of various denominations, a dozen or so pubs with interesting histories, almshouses such as those surviving at Greenhead, small houses hiding their medieval origins, and numerous small shops, cottages and workshops that have gone through untold conversions. Just a few of these – most still surviving – captured by the camera in the last 100 years have been selected for inclusion here.

Cowley Manor, a late sixteenth or early seventeenth century house built by the Earl of Shrewsbury. It replaced a medieval manor house described by a seventeenth century historian as 'a stately castle-like house moated about'. The house was the centre of a large estate which included land at Thorpe Hesley and Shirecliffe in Sheffield.

Ancient cruck barn at Cowley Manor, now demolished. Cruck buildings were once common in the area not only for barns but also for substantial residential buildings.

Durants' Garage in the 1920s. It stood where Chapeltown Garage now stands. Smith Street can be seen in the right background.

Chapeltown Garage about 1960 – bigger than Durants' but still prefabricated. In the background is Parramore's Foundry and on the far left is an area of allotments known as California Gardens.

Ellis's shop at Chapeltown about 1895 (see page 12). As can be seen from the sign, this business had been built up by offering a wide-ranging service extending from men's and boys', and women's and girls' clothing, to boots and shoes, furniture and wallpaper. Hats and dresses were made on the premises. The title of the premises, 'Manchester House' reflects their specialisation in cotton goods. Standing at the entrance to the shop are the proprietors, Mr and Mrs Lewis, their staff and their children. Mrs Lewis was the daughter of the founder of the business, Mr Charles Ellis. Standing in front of Mrs Lewis is their son Harold who died in 1972 aged 85.

Ivy House, Chapeltown. This house stood behind Gibson's store (see page 10) and was the residence of Thomas Chambers and his descendants the Gibsons who ran the store after his death. The house later became the headquarters of Chapeltown Scouts and then Chapeltown Dramatic Society. It was demolished in the 1920s and part of its site is now occupied by the garden and part of the forecourt of the Newton Hall.

Chapeltown House in 1925. This late seventeenth or early eighteenth century house was associated with a succession of prominent Chapeltown residents from the early eighteenth century including the Allen family (who owned it for about 200 years), Matthew Chambers, a grandson of one of the founders of Newton Chambers, George Dawson, manager of Thorncliffe Ironworks, and Charles Ellis, the clothes retailer.

The Picture Palace, Chapeltown. Purpose-built in the Moorish style, in red brick with a white stucco front, it was opened on 23 December 1912. The capacity then was about 700. There were shows every evening at 6.30 and 8.30 with admission charges of 3d in the pit, 4d in the saloon and 6d in the stalls. There was a children's matinee at 2.30 p.m. on Saturdays. The opening programme included *The Redemption of Ben Farland* (a western) and *Grandma's Sleeping Draught* (a comedy). Music was provided by a trio of piano, violin and double bass. The cinema went over to 'talkies' in January 1931. A remarkable feature of the Picture Palace was that it had the same chief projectionist, Alfred Dawson, from the day it opened in 1912 until 1954! The final film programme was a double feature: *Lone Star* and *King Solomon's Mines* on Saturday 16 March 1963. Three days later the hall was re-opened as the Palace Casino with Star Bingo.

Chapeltown Co-op, Station Road in the early 1900s.This was a large emporium which offered stiff competition to local independent shopkeepers. At that period the branch contained grocery, drapery, boots and butchering departments.

Station Road Primitive Methodist Chapel (built 1884) in the early 1900s, wedged between the Commercial Hotel and shops including W. Brock's watch and clock maker's and jewellery store.

Whitaker's pawnbrokers, Station Road, Chapeltown. The photograph shows the owner and his assistant. Among the many items on display are carpets, rugs, boots and shoes, flat caps, socks and leather belts. The rolled-up floral carpet above the shop doorway is marked '9/- Great Bargain'. The framed picture immediately to the right of the shop assistant is marked '10/- Great Bargain.'

Housley Hall in a state of disrepair. The ancient manor of Howsley is recorded as early as 1436 when it was owned by John Howsley and his wife Joan. It remained in the Housley or Housley Freeman families until 1837 when it came into the hands of Right Hon. James Stuart Wortley who sold it to his cousin the Earl of Wharncliffe. The Hall, which still stands, dates from the seventeenth century. Since 1837 the Hall has had a chequered history being at various times the home of members of the Chambers family (of Newton Chambers), a boys' boarding school (there were thirty boarders there in 1841 when the schoolmaster was Samuel Warburton), and various farming tenants including Joseph Moulson, Wilfred Hartley, Ernest Barnes, and finally the Kennington brothers. It has since been restored as a private residence.

Greenhead Almshouses and, in the background, Greenhead Wesleyan Reform Chapel. The almshouses were founded by Mrs Ann Freeman, the last of the Freeman family of Housley Hall in 1837. The almshouses were designed to be occupied by six persons, each with their own front door. In the centre of the building, distinguished by its castellated appearance, is a communal room used as a reading room and chapel. The almshouses are now occupied by Winn and Cooper, Solicitors.

Lane End Workmen's Club. This building was erected in 1864 and demolished in 1972. It was designed as a club for the workmen of Newton Chambers at Thorncliffe. During the lockout of 1869/70 a company of Royal Dublin Fusiliers was billeted here to keep the peace in the district.

Old Barnes Hall from an illustration in John Eastwood's *History of Ecclesfield* (1862). Built in the first half of the fourteenth century it was demolished in 1823. Between 1498 and 1823 it was in the Scott and Watts families (who were related). The first Scott was Thomas Scott (also known as Thomas Rotherham, who was Archbishop of York (he died in 1500).

The new Barnes Hall erected in 1824 by William Smith, the new proprietor of the Barnes Hall estate. The new mansion was built to the south of the site of the old hall which he had demolished the previous year. William Smith, who had married Elizabeth Parkyn of Mortomley Hall, had previously lived at Cowley Manor. The house was occupied continuously from 1824 until 1956 by members of the Smith family. Perhaps the best-known member of the family was Lady Mabel Smith, daughter of Earl Fitzwilliam, who married William Mackenzie Smith in 1899.

Lane End Almshouses founded by Edward Sylvester who conveyed land in 1693 to pay for the building of the almshouses and the provision of pensions for their occupants. The almshouses consisted of 'seven rooms for seven poor men or women of the Parish of Ecclesfield, respect being had to those who live on the north side of the Parish'. The occupants were to receive at least 30 shillings a year. The building has been demolished and part of Copley House now occupies the site.

Angram Bank Farm, Thompson Hill, about 1900. Mr Gore the farmer is standing in the doorway. This farm, like others in the district, has disappeared under the relentless spread of suburbanisation.

Regulars outside The Salutation Inn at High Green in the early 1920s (see also page 28).

The Rose Inn, Potter Hill, before the First World War when it was a beerhouse.

The Travellers' Inn, Thompson Hill (see also page 27). This public house stood on the corner of Thompson Hill and Potter Hill Lane. The landlord, Tom Beet, is the shirt-sleeved figure standing by the window. The old pub is now a dwelling house.

A group at the back of the Travellers' Inn, Thompson Hill early this century.

1. Unknown, 2. unknown, 3. unknown, 4. unknown, 5. Tom Marsh, 6. Albert Dransfield, 7. Jim Steele, 8. Dick Sellars, 9. Walter Dearden, 10. Joe Kaye, 11. Theo Dransfield, 12. Harry Dransfield, 13. Charles Whittington, 14. Frank Rodgers, 15. Parkin Steele, 16. Tom Ashton, 17. ? Southern, 18. George Dransfield, 19. Tommy Dransfield, 20. Tommy Vickers, 21. Walter Kaye, 22. Bill Hutchinson, 23. William Henry Gledhill, 24. Burt Biggins, 25. George Ashton, 26. unknown, 27. Tom Steele, 28. Herbert Shaw, 29. unknown, 30. unknown, 31. Jane Ann Dransfield, 32. unknown, 33. unknown, 34. unknown, 35. unknown.

Bridge Houses, Westwood. These old cottages, belonging to Newton Chambers, were located in Thorncliffe Wood. The track in the background led to the Great Central Railway line which crossed the track on a bridge.

Warren Co-operative Store. The first Co-operative store in the Chapeltown and High Green area was established on Warren Lane. The first store was in the cottage belonging to William and Elizabeth Vernon, their bedroom acting as flour chamber and their kitchen as shop and storeroom. The store then moved to larger rented premises until the store featured in the photograph was built about 1900.

Three

Portraits

A community's character is a distillation of its locality (upland, rolling countryside, coast) its resources (good soil, timber, coal, iron) and its people. In the earliest times people living in the Chapeltown and High Green area farmed the land, exploited the woods and quarried stone. From the mid-sixteenth century ironstone and charcoal (from the local woods) gave rise to a small iron manufacturing industry but it was not until the rapid growth of Newton Chambers' works at Thorncliffe in the early nineteenth century that substantial numbers of migrants from other regions were attracted to the district. By the end of the nineteenth century there were people living in the district from every corner of Great Britain and Ireland. The portraits that follow – formal and informal, of individuals and families, of locals and incomers, young and old, at work and at leisure – have been selected to reflect the contribution made by thousands of individuals to the forging of the district's distinctive character.

George Newton (1761-1825). In partnership with Thomas Chambers (1761-1817), George Newton founded the Thorncliffe Ironworks in December 1793. Newton combined a shrewd and efficient control of the company's finances with an evangelical zeal for Wesleyan Methodism which he was instrumental in introducing into the district. Throughout his life he suffered from bouts of increasingly severe deafness, a condition curiously emphasised by his pose in this portrait.

A group at the opening ceremony of a new laboratory at the Thorncliffe Works in 1937. On the left with the walking stick is Sir Harold West and in the centre wearing the homburg hat is Sir Samuel Roberts.

Staff of Sagars' butcher's shop at Chapeltown with, left to right, William Sagar, Charlie Wetherall, Fred Mallinson and Joe Sagar.

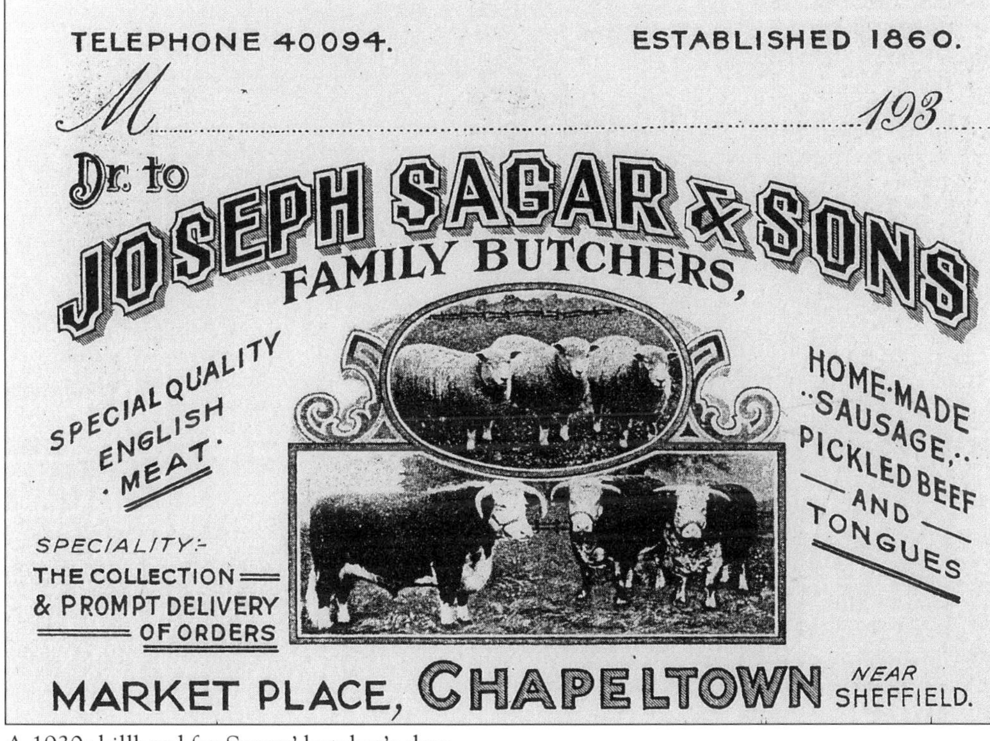

A 1930s billhead for Sagars' butcher's shop.

Women's Voluntary Service (WVS) outside Staindrop Lodge, Thorncliffe, in the 1940s, knitting for victory.

Members of Chapeltown Red Cross with Newton Chambers medical and First Aid staff taken about 1946.

A fine studio portrait of Mabel Frances Westerman (1883-1952). She was born at Hall Wood Side, the daughter of Joseph and Clara Westerman. She was a pupil teacher at Burncross School (see page 90) before she married Arnold Warburton, who became Secretary to Mr Newton of Newton Chambers. She was a stalwart member of both Burncross and Mt. Pleasant chapels.

The brothers Benjamin Arnold Greaves, John Ernest Greaves and Harry Greaves. B.A. Greaves was born at Charlton Clough, Bracken Hill in 1866. He was trained as a cabinet maker at the family's workshop where one of the specialities was making the cases for grandfather clocks. After sailing to Tasmania in a wind-jammer, he returned to concentrate on the fast-growing art of photography and steadily made a good local reputation. The photographs on pages 56 (bottom), 57 and 97(bottom) are by B.A. Greaves.

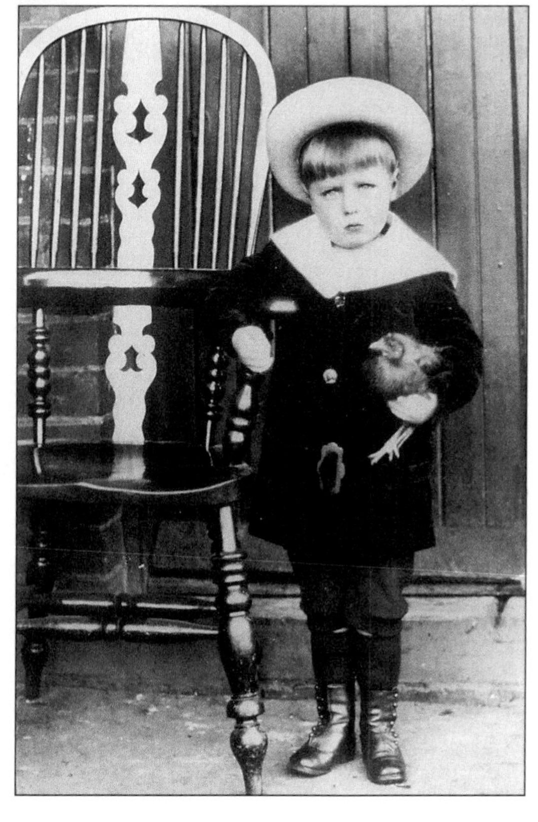

Herbert Greaves with his pet pullet – which later went into the pot! Herbert was the youngest of five children of George and Sarah Greaves who kept a shop at Charlton Brook. The bird was eaten with relish by father, while the children looked on unable to choke down a morsel.

In 1928 George Ellis was appointed chief chemist at the newly-built Smithywood Coking Plant. In the same year he married Dorothy Beard at St John's church, Chapeltown. Dorothy's twin sister Phyll, who was a Tiller girl performing at the Moulin Rouge in Paris was unable to attend the wedding so instead she sent a special gift, Dorothy's wedding dress – Parisian chic in Chapeltown!

A well posed Victorian family studio portrait. Mrs Caroline Binks, seated, was born in 1839 and died in 1927. Mrs Binks, born Caroline Lax, married first Robert Kirk, a migrant from Scotland, who was a moulder at Newton Chambers, but who died at the age of 38. Standing in the centre is Priscilla Kirk, their daughter. As a young widow with three children Mrs Kirk took on a variety of jobs including nursing, waiting at table at functions and taking in medical students as paying guests. She re-married to Noah Binks, a carter from Chapeltown. One of their three daughters stands on the left.

Mary French, daughter of Jack and Alice French, stands proudly with her new pram and dolls on the edge of Hall Wood in the early 1930s. For over a century three generations of the French family were blacksmiths at Grenoside and Charlton Clough.

The Stutchbury family of Mafeking Street, Lound Side in the early 1900s. The parents, seated on the left and right were Anna Elizabeth and George. George was a coalminer at the Old Thorncliffe Drift. The children were, standing at the back, left to right, Charlie, Muriel, Edgar, Evelyn and Cecil, and at the front, Frank, Dora and Freda. Edgar was among the Thorncliffe workers who installed a semi-water gas plant in the Soviet Union in the early 1930s (see page 79).

Edith, Norah, Amy and Grace Prior of Charlton Brook in *c.* 1925 in their home-made gingham dresses and knitted socks.

Chapeltown Park Bandstand and Memorial Committee, 1925.

The wedding of Edward Fearnley Ellam and Lucy Smith, 22 September, 1910. Left to right are Herbert Smith, brother of the bride, Clarice Cooney, niece of the bride, the groom and bride, Henry Steel, best man, and Elsie Cooney, niece of the bride. Herbert Smith was a moulder at Thorncliffe Ironworks and lived on Thorncliffe Lane until his death in 1944. The Cooney girls were daughters of Fred Cooney who was a well known engineer with Newton Chambers (Manchester) who installed kitchen equipment and heating systems throughout the country. The groom was a wages clerk at Newton Chambers, and the bride was a class teacher and then head teacher at High Green Board School. The groom died in 1918 at the early age of 39 and Mrs Ellam returned to her school teaching career, initially at High Green, and afterwards at Lound Infant School where she remained until her retirement through illness in 1928. She died in 1934. An interesting feature of the photograph, is that the photographer – B.A. Greaves – has obliterated another guest, John Hobson, a lodger at the bride's family home, who was standing in the doorway and who would have spoiled the composition of the group. However, his watch chain and polished boot can still be seen!

Mrs Anne Rice (*née* Bennett), High Green's midwife. This photograph was taken in about 1910 with her grandsons Fred, John and Tom.

George Edwin Worthey (d. 1950) of High Green on army service in May 1916. George's father, Edwin, kept a gentlemen's outfitters and general store on Wortley Road, which later became a Barnsley British Co-operative Store. It is now a mini-market.

A group of customers and friends outside High Green Working Men's Club early this century. On the extreme right (with folded arms) is Mr Lawton the caretaker, his wife and their daughter Elsie.

In the billiards and snooker room at High Green Working Men's Club. At the table is Mr Lawton the caretaker, watched by Mrs Lawton (centre) and Mr and Mrs Marshall.

Mrs Ann Champion (born 1775). This is a water-colour portrait painted in 1858. Mrs Champion was the mother-in-law of Thomas Chapman, filecutter and landlord of the Acorn Inn at Bracken Hill. The painting was one of three family portraits (the others were of the men and boys of the family and of the women and girls) possibly painted by an itinerant artist.

The Bidwell family of Howbrook.

George Elliott (1832-1915), a pit deputy from High Green. This studio portrait was taken in the 1880s.

William Lee (1843-1916), miner of Howbrook. The Lee family lived in Primrose Cottage, a one-up-one-down dwelling, which still stands today.

Lucy (*née* Dransfield) and William Lee with their thirteen children in their cottage garden at Howbrook. Standing, left to right, are Samuel, Jane, Laura, Agnes, James, Annie, Bertha, Elizabeth, Edward, Mary Harriet and George; sitting at the front are Ernest (left) and Albert (right).

Miners on a Sunday morning walk. The moustached figure with the clay pipe is Albert Dransfield who appears in the group at the Travellers' Inn (page 45). Note the miners' 'squat'.

Hello sailor! The Hulbert boys of Warren Lane.

Cottage fireside. One of the original photographs that came into the possession of Chapeltown and High Green Archive on the death of local amateur photographer, Alan Boulton.

George Dickinson, John Willie Wilcock and Martin Dickinson in their Sunday suits.

Sarah Smith (*née* Windle) in about 1880. She was born in 1835 and died in 1930, just before her 95th birthday. Before her marriage she was in service to Samuel Plimsoll (the originator of the Plimsoll line on ships) who was associated with Newton Chambers and lived in Sheffield. She had eleven children of whom nine reached adulthood. She was a strict disciplinarian and sabbatarian. Her grandson recalls that he could not paint on a Sunday but could draw, and could only play hymns on the piano.

Sarah Smith with two of her daughters, Marion (behind her) and Bertha (in front of her) and Marion's friend, Peggy Norman, on holiday at Scarborough in 1906.

James Watson Almond and Ann Jane Almond, both seated, after the christening of their son John Duff Almond in 1896. Frances Almond, James's sister is standing behind the proud parents. The Almonds kept the Miners' Arms at Warren from 1899 until about 1926.

Four

Thorncliffe Works

Newton Chambers & Co, of Thorncliffe Ironworks, dominated the economic and social life of the district for 180 years. The firm, which was established at Thorncliffe in December 1793, employed men and boys, and, latterly girls and women in a bewildering variety of jobs. The firm operated, at one time or another, collieries, ironstone pits, limestone quarries, coke ovens, blast furnaces, foundries, excavator plants, chemical works, paper works and bottling plants. The company also ran their own farms to provide grazing and foodstuffs for the many horses and ponies that they employed in their collieries and around their works. By 1900 it employed more than 8,000 workpeople. This complex industrial enterprise was supported by wide-ranging training and welfare initiatives, by workers' housing and by the provision of a wide range of cultural and sporting opportunities. After trading independently for 180 years, the firm was taken over by Central & Sheerwood in 1973 and gradually sold off. Now, apart from office buildings that have been incorporated into a new industrial park, little evidence remains of what was one of the giants of the Industrial Revolution in South Yorkshire.

Thorncliffe Works *c.* 1825. In this view the original blast furnaces of 1795 and 1796 can be seen protruding from behind the sloping roof of the foundry in the centre of the picture. The works originally manufactured a huge range of small castings such as anvils, stoves, pans, boot scrapers, sash-weights and gutters, but by 1815 had diversified into heavy castings. The circular, kiln-shaped building on the right was the Rotunda, or casting house, which on the 19 July 1820 was the scene of an accident which cost the lives of eight workmen and George Newton's son, Isaac. A five-ton girder for Southwark Bridge was being cast in a 15 feet-deep pit when the sand-packed lower box exploded and the Rotunda was filled with showers of molten metal. Beside the Rotunda, the chimney of the steam engine house (which provided the cold blast of air for the furnaces) is belching smoke, and in the background horse-drawn wagons may be seen bringing ironstone and coke ready for barrowing into the furnaces. The two figures in the foreground are standing on the bank of the Blackburn Brook.

Thorncliffe Works in the 1940s, looking in a north-easterly direction across the Blackburn Brook valley. In the foreground is Thorncliffe Lane leading down into the works (see also page 24). On either side of Thorncliffe Lane the ground shows the typical disturbance associated with early mining. The long, two storied white building off to the right of the bottom of Thorncliffe Lane is the 'White House', the main office block. The extensive areas of workshops on the left are camouflaged against air attack. In the left background leading off Warren Lane (shown by the linear grouping of houses in the right background) is the 'tank factory' (see pages 83 and 84).

Thorncliffe Works in its heyday was surrounded and criss-crossed by a complex system of railways for moving raw materials and products into, about and away from the works. This photograph shows one of the firm's shunting locomotives. Most of the Thorncliffe locomotives carried local names, including Chapeltown, Norfolk, Thorncliffe, Staindrop and Mortomley.

The locomotives could also be put to other uses! In this case a loco is being used to convey Yorkshire MPs around the works in 1943.

Part of a *Luftwaffe* photograph of the Thorncliffe Works and surrounding area taken in 1940 which was found in the map room of a German Air Force station near Bremen at the end of the Second World War. The air photo was entitled *Eisenwerk* 'Thorncliffe Jronworks Newton Chambers u. Co. Ltd.' The works complex is enclosed within the thick black line and each department clearly numbered and, in a separate key, named in detail. Whoever did the numbering probably came to Thorncliffe in the years immediately before the war. One local resident remembered some Germans advising on the modernisation of the foundry in the 1930s. The spy must have been there before 1938 when work began on the tank factory (the building in the field to the north-east of the number 5) because this important Churchill Tank factory was overlooked. It is a bit unnerving to see beside the Burncross Road an arrow pointing south and the words 'Nach Sheffield mitte etwa 9 km luftlinie' (central Sheffield 9 kilometres as the crow flies).

Part of the Newton Chambers war effort through National War Savings. Sir Harold West, Managing Director, is on the left.

Thorncliffe Home Guard unit. Back row, left to right: Jack Wright, Jim Rice, -?-. Next row: Alf Fletcher, Herbert Pinder, Cyril Bywater, Dick Trickett, Harry Moore, ? Ogle, Frank Lynch. Next row: C. Bennett, Dick Hindley, Joe Martin, Johnny Goddard, John Woodhead, A. Denton, Charlie Peace, Richie Sunderland. Front row: Ralph Morris, Captain Smith, J. Robertson, William Pickering, L. Bee, ? Barker.

Miners at Smithy Wood Colliery reading a new government poster underlining the need to maximise coal output to provide fuel for convoys.

Mining apprentices, 1943. Sir Harold West had initiated an innovative youth training scheme in 1942 called 'The Thorncliffe Experiment'. Among other things it included a 'sandwich scheme' with trainees having one month in six at the training centre. The scheme attracted much attention from politicians, educationalists and industrialists.

One of the two blast furnaces erected in 1873-74. Pig iron was made at Thorncliffe from 1795 until 1942. The first two blast furnaces were erected in 1795 and 1796. These were replaced in 1873-74. The mid-Victorian furnaces, together with a third built in 1913, were evenually replaced by a mechanised furnace built in 1927.

Blast Furnace workmen, 1906. Back row, left to right: Thomas O'Hara, William Luckett, George B. Hughes, Willaim C. Windle, Thomas Kelly. Front row: William Housley, David Hunt, William Merritt, Frank Redfern. David Hunt was the hoist man and worked the hoist which elevated the ore, coke and limestone to the top of the furnace. William Windle acted as liaison between the blast furnace manager and the fillers when changes had to be made in the charges to the furnace. The remaining seven men were employed as fillers. They conveyed the raw materials in barrows from the heaps of ore and coke on Furnace Hill. They all worked twelve hour shifts with a double shift on alternate Sundays.

Moulders in the Heavy Castings Department preparing moulds for coke oven castings.

Harry Yale in the Heavy Castings Department.

An Aveling and Porter single cylinder traction engine preparing to haul salt pans from Thorncliffe to a chemical works in Northwich, Cheshire, in 1916.

A large ladle ready to be transported to a customer on a Scammell low-loader in 1938. The figure on the left is Harry Westnedge. The blast furnace which was demolished in 1942 is in the background.

Newton Chambers employees and Russian workers at Bobriki near Moscow in 1932 in connection with a contract to supply and erect a semi-water gas plant at a steelworks. Sitting on the tank are Douglas Hirst on the right and Frank Chambers next to him. Standing on the extreme left is Mr Rees, next to Nina the Russian interpreter. All the others are Russians except for the bareheaded man standing on the right who was a contract worker from Leicester. The late George Smith, who was working on the contract but is not in the photograph, graphically recalled details of his time there. The party from Newton Chambers travelled overland to Bobriki – a distance of 1,700 miles. When they arrived in the Soviet Union their passports were taken away 'presumably to discourage us from straying'. They were accommodated in a hotel in a temporary township, along with Americans and Germans, who were working on related contracts. The foreign workers were waited on day and night, George Smith recalled, and he soon found that bars of Izal soap acted as an incentive for waitresses. The erection of the plant was carried out seven days a week and rota days were taken off in turn. On their return journey they were lined up at Minsk railway station and one member of the party had to return to Moscow to have a passport irregularity sorted out.

Albert Noble in his blacksmith's shop at Thorncliffe.

The interior of the old Chapel Furnace which was acquired by Newton Chambers in 1860. Paving slabs and kerb stones were manufactured here in the 1920s using cement and crushed furnace slag. The Izal factory was later built on the site.

Car Transporter. Ted Dye, shown in the photograph, recalls that Newton Chambers started making car transporters for the Eastern Region of British Railways in the late 1950s. 'They were mainly home-designed and home-made in the machine, fitting and construction shops. The early testing of the transporter's strength in the event of an accident was a bit of a Heath Robinson job. It was pulled up an incline and then allowed to run freely down into a line of stationary wagons, hopefully with little or no damage to the cars. The transporters were maintained by Newton Chambers' men who used to go down to work in the railway sidings which ran alongside the Caledonian Road in London. They stayed in "colourful" lodgings nearby – quite an entertaining experience.'

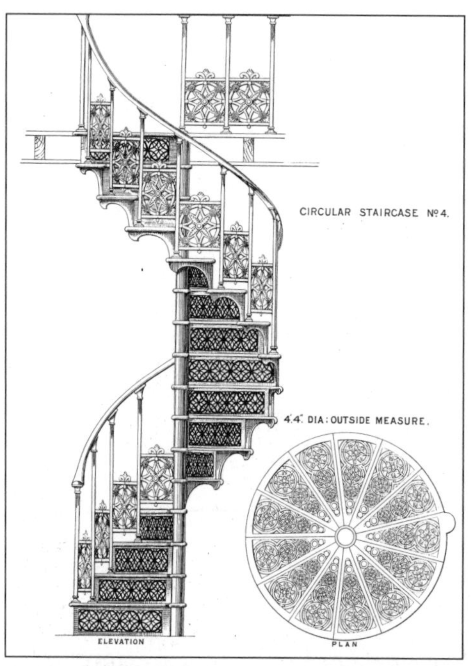

Cast iron production at Thorncliffe in the nineteenth and early twentieth centuries covered a bewildering variety of products. This illustration shows an intricate spiral staircase featured in an undated nineteenth century pattern book.

The 'Thorncliffe' cooking range. Newton Chambers were renowned for their Yorkshire ranges. This stove included two ovens at the top, with a plate rack between; a large hot plate for frying, stewing and grilling, and at the bottom, on either side of the fire, two 'hot closets'.

At the end of the First World War, Newton Chambers' ammunitions business disappeared almost overnight. In an attempt to create employment, replace lost markets and contribute to the house building programme, the production of cast iron houses was begun. The photograph shows some of the first houses being built in Mortomley Close.

The Tank Factory, Warren Lane. Construction began in 1938 for excavator production but before it was completed the Second World War began, and it became a major assembly plant for Churchill tanks – 1,160 were built there. After the war it resumed its role as an excavator plant.

A Churchill tank on test. Sir Harold West stands on the left.

Testing an NCK 304 dragshovel at the test ground on Warren Lane. NCK machines were made under licence from Koehring & Co. of Milwaukee under an agreement signed in 1946. These dragshovels were used on the opencast coal sites at nearby Wentworth.

Craft apprentices and apprentice draughtsmen, August 1960. Alan Thorpe, fifth from the right in the middle row, remembers that leather belts were worn at the waist to indicate new entrants. Note books and pens were kept in top pockets to make notes of anything important during lectures, visits and demonstrations.

Graham Cawthorne, draughtsman, 1949.

Thorncliffe office staff in the early 1950s. Back row, left to right: Jessie Hollin, Jean Deakin. Front row, left to right: Evelyn Agnes Archer (Head of Tracing Office), Hazel Shaw, Pat McDool, Nora Schofield, Christine Harrison, Mabel Rollins.

Staff of the Managers' Dining Room.

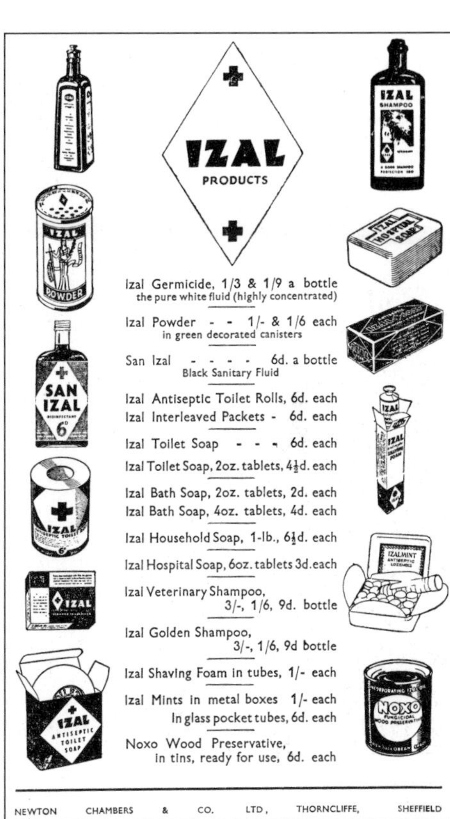

The story of Izal, Newton Chambers' most famous product, began in 1885 when J.H. Worrall was taken on to analyse the by-products of the firm's coke ovens. The oxidised portion of the oils was repeatedly distilled until a germicidal oil was produced. It was first marketed as a sheep dip until in 1893 the trade name 'Izal' was patented. By 1900 Izal disinfectant was being used in base and field hospitals in the Boer War for the treatment of dysentery. There was an amazing range of Izal products from disinfectants, soaps and shampoos to lozenges and mints. Toilet roll production began in the 1920s, at first simply to advertise the range of Izal products. The advert is from the *Rotherham Advertiser* in 1939.

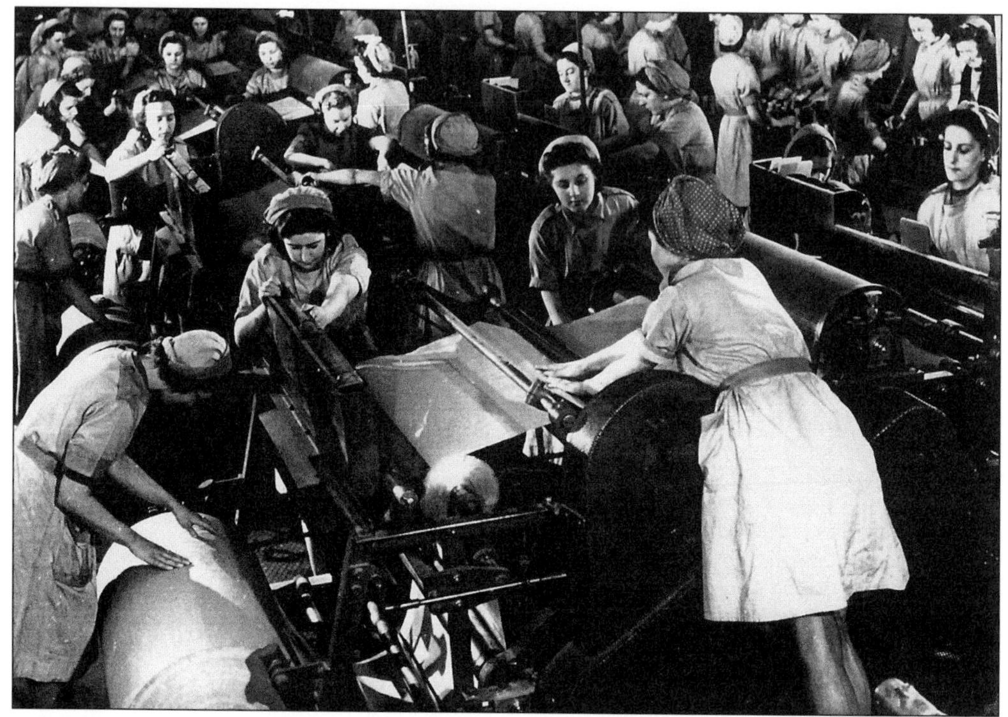

Labour-intensive production lines in the Izal Paper Factory.

Izal staff on the roof of the factory waiting for King George VI and Queen Elizabeth to pass on Station Road, Chapeltown in 1938.

Five

Schooldays

In the early 1840s when the sub-commissioner for the Children's Employment Commission (Mines) came to High Green he was scathing in his condemnation of the provision for the education of local children. He described a dame school, which was cold and damp and also used as a storehouse for faggots. He said 'to talk of education would be a mockery in such a place'. He went on to say that the only other education in High Green was provided by 'an old cripple who is a wiseman of the country... and who not only tells fortunes but who is widely famed for supernatural craft touching missing bodies, stolen goods and stray pigs.' He went on to say that beyond this very poor provision the children could attend 'distant Sunday-schools'. A school existed at the top of Lound, founded in 1716, and rebuilt in 1844 as a National School. High Green School, on Wortley Road, was built in 1843 with money raised by voluntary subscriptions and grants from the British and Foreign Society. Following the 1870 Education Act, Board Schools were also established at Burncross, Lound and Warren and, with the exception of those living at Howbrook and Westwood Rows who had a longish walk, most children in the district were then within a short distance of a free education.

Staff of Burncross School *c.* 1900. On the front row, right, is pupil teacher Mabel Westerman (see page 51).

Miss Tantum's class, Burncross Infants, at the harvest festival in 1954.

Miss Mathewman's class, Burncross School, 1927. Back row, left to right: Bacon, Cope, Hattersley, Bert Goddard, Ronnie Brooks, Lewis Shaw, Dougy Laycock, Edith Hattersley, Joan Gradwell. Next to back row: Mr Platts (head teacher), Harry Ashton, Joe Brammah, Gordon Ogden, George Forweather, -?-, Arthur Page, -?-, Nellie Brook, Miss Mathewman. Middle row: Edna Rushworth, Margaret Arthur, Letty Wombwell, Marian Deighton, Jane Dearden, -?-, Alice Parrott, -?-, Annie Gilberthorpe, Lizzie Charlesworth. Next to front row: Doris Hollingsworth, Joyce Brook, Elsie Burtoft, Lena Kay, Laura Hoyland, Phyllis Hattersley, Mary Padley, Joan Kirkham. Front row: Eric Belk, Shaw, Clifford Jenkinson, Amy Prior, Ellis Kirk, Parken Hullett, Ernest Platts, Elsie Gibson, Frank Locking.

Lound Council School, Standard 6, 1928.

Greengate Lane School, 1931-32. The class teacher is Mr Fulleylove.

Staff of High Green Secondary Modern School, 1952. Back row, left to right: Mrs Plant, Dennis Hughes, A. Legge, Dorothy Clough, E. Siletto, A. Eyre, B. Oxley, C.B. Rudkin, Joan Gradwell, H. Fulleylove. Front row: C. Bennett, Margaret Woolley, A. Gledhill, E. Staines, Frank Piper (head teacher), G. Williams, Mr Johnson, J. Monteyne, I. Wilkinson.

Warren Council School, Standard 4A and 5, 1928. Back row, left to right: Tom Steel, Cliff Bell, Doug Bennett, Mabel Ruder, Elsie Denton, Tessie Watkinson, Madge Burgin, Winnie Hobson, Eric Burgin, Frank Burgin, Len Jenkinson. Next to back row: Ron Chapman, Ralph Fields, Reg Scampton, Win Lovelock, Alberta Merritt, Gladys Smith, Kathy Watkinson, Mary Butcher, Richard Whiteley, A. Lowery, H. Watkinson. Next row: H. Scampton, Doug Rollings, R. Bellamy, Hilda Taylor, Eleanor Steel, Doris Cotterill, A. Newbold, Irene Sharpe, P. Sherriff, Cliff Parry, Geoff Smith. Front row: E. Sutton, J. Kirk, Albert Rollings, Doug Green, Dolly Slack, Joyce Crossland, Sybill Cole, Roebuck, Ron Saffell, Ralph Stutchberry, H. Barber, John Deaton. The teacher is Mr Sykes.

A class at Warren Infants in 1910.

Six

Churches and Chapels

Before 1860, the Chapeltown and High Green area lay in three ecclesiastical parishes: most of the area lay within Ecclesfield parish, one of the biggest parishes in England; the Westwood area lay in Tankersley parish; and Howbrook was in Wortley parish. This meant a long walk to the parish church for most parishioners. Ecclesfield parish was gradually dismembered and drastically reduced in size. In the Chapeltown and High Green parts of the parish, St John's church was established to serve Chapeltown in 1860 and St Saviour's to serve High Green was built in 1872. The Westwood Rows were served by a mission church from the mother church at Tankersley. Superimposed on this new pattern of Anglican provision was a network of non-conformist congregations in chapels at Warren, Potter Hill, Stoneygate and Wortley Road at High Green, and Burncross, Mt. Pleasant, Greenhead and Station Road at Chapeltown. A strong Methodist tradition was developed in the area, partly through the early efforts of the founders of Newton Chambers, who were staunch Methodists who recruited workmen through Methodist channels in other areas. A Catholic church was later established at High Green. One of the highlights of the year until recently was the annual Whit Gathering and Sing with followings from all the Anglican and non-conformist churches in the district.

Mount Pleasant Methodist Chapel built in 1866 on the site of the original Mount Pleasant Chapel which was opened in 1806. This chapel is now closed.

The interior of Mount Pleasant Methodist Church.

The Mission Church at Westwood. This church which belonged to the parish church at Tankersley, served the outlying settlement at the Westwood Rows (see page 29).

An interior view of Mortomley St Saviour's church. It is decorated for a harvest festival. This church was built in 1872 as a memorial to Parkin Jeffcock who lost his life whilst trying to rescue miners who were trapped in the Oakes Colliery, Barnsley, after an explosion.

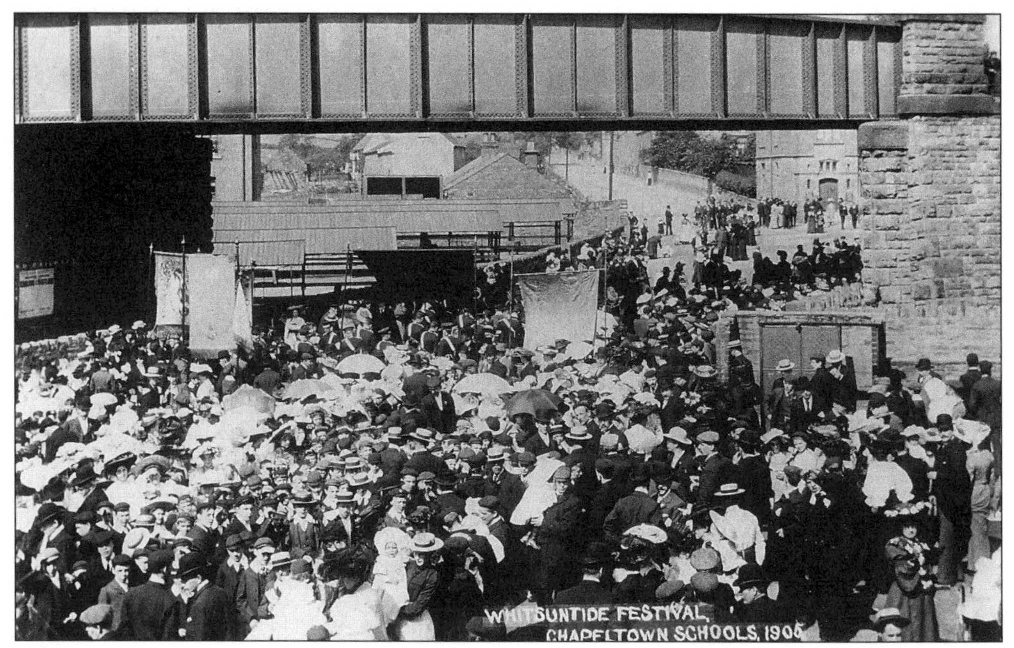

Whitsuntide gathering under the Midland Railway bridge at Chapeltown in 1905 prior to the march to the Ten Acre.

Combined High Green and Chapeltown churches and chapels Whit sing at the Ten Acre in 1930. The Thorncliffe Works form a dramatic backdrop.

Whit sing at Barnes Hall in the 1950s. Traditionally Burncross Methodist Chapel went to sing at Barnes Hall on Whit Sunday. After the sing the children were given an iced bun with a cherry on the top and an orange.

Sunday School queens in Chapeltown Park at Whitsuntide in the late 1950s. On the right are the Revd and Mrs Frank Gouge of St John's church, Chapeltown.

Induction service of the Revd O.R. Craze at St Saviour's church at Mortomley. Back row, left to right: -?-, Taylor, M. Crisp, J. Greenwood, J. Woodward, D. Crisp, S. Robinson, -?-, J. Kaye, -?-, -?-, -?-, -?-. Middle row: G. Bennett, Taylor, B. Codd, -?-, D. Payne, G. Forrester, B. Davies, T. Payne, -?-, -?-, S. Johnson, -?-. Front row: Robinson, Kilner, Wilkinson, -?-, Johnson, -?-, Revd Craze (Senior), Revd O.R. Craze, A. Sansam, Armitage, Greenwood, -?-, Sansam, P. Sansam.

St Saviour's church, Mortomley (see also page 97).

Seven

Leisure Time

The cultural life of the Chapeltown and High Green area was – and continues to be – remarkably rich and varied. It ranges from the family with its seasonal gatherings and visitings, to the informal community of the street which came together on special occasions, and formal organisations like the church and chapel, working men's club, concert party, operatic society, brass band and a myriad of sporting clubs. The Thorncliffe Works had an immense influence on cultural and sporting activity through its network of works-sponsored teams and other 'after work' provision. In this section we have tried to capture images of a representative range of leisure pursuits, cultural activities and other public gatherings and private get-togethers, mostly from the first sixty years of the century.

Thorncliffe Drawing Office Cricket Team *c.* 1949. Back row includes Graham Cawthorne, B. Burkinshaw, Eric Dixon. Front row, left to right: Norman Burrows, R. Middleton, -?-, Geoff Athey, G. Taylor, F. Fisher, J.V. Hague, Bill Ruddlesden.

Thorncliffe Recreational Association Football Club, Drake League Champions – Season 1953/54. Back row, left to right: D. Smith, G. Platts, D. Schofield, D. Moore, D. Childs, A. Hill, G. Morris. Front row: B. Goddard, P. Lynch, R. Parrot (Capt), B. Straw, P. Roach, E. Holman.

Warren Wesleyan Sunday Schools' two football teams in the early 1930s. Back row, left to right: F. Eyre, Harry Evans (Chairman and head master of Warren School), Harold Eyre, W. Vernon, Reg Braham, H. Biggins, J. Grant (referee), T. Slack, F. Hoyland. Next to back row: W. Hill (goalkeeper and secretary), J. Marshall, C. Eyre, G. Sanderson, L. Lambert, T. Marshall. Next row: H. Bennett (trainer), G. Newbold, G. Kelly, M. Chambers, T. Whitham, F. Denton, E. Hague, R. Stutchberry, W. Smith, L. Ashton, C. Bennett, Bernard Eyre (trainer). Front row: G. Galloway (president), V. Garton, A. Steel, A. Whitham, F. French, E. Hutchinson, Arnie Mellor, W. Clare, H. Varley, A. Grant. Bernard Eyre's mother was caretaker at the Chapel and she washed and ironed all the twenty-two kits every week and made sure the teams had a cup of coffee at half-time.

Mount Pleasant Tennis team with the Oughtibridge team before the First World War.

Warren Junior School Rounders team, 1951.

Fishing trip from the Thorncliffe Arms, Warren at the Loggerheads Inn *c.* 1910.

Sports Day at Thorncliffe in the late 1950s.

High Green Senior Scout Troop, 1956, proudly displaying the Wentworth District Senior Scout Trophy. Standing, left to right: Michael Cooper, Denis Smith, David Crisp. Kneeling: John Vickers and Stuart Rodgers.

Scouts and guides marching down Wortley Road, High Green, during the Second World War.

High Green Youth Orchestra, 1957. Back row, left to right: Tony Ellis, Jennie Morris, others are unknown except for Bill Scott (teacher, with violin) and Mr F. Piper (Head teacher, on the right). Middle row: Maurice Brown, Roy Denton, Derek Renshaw, David Frost, Connie Kitson, Neil Brookes, then on the far right, David Flather. Front row: Jean Bee, Marjorie Scholey, -?-, Ivan Martin.

Chapeltown Silver Prize Band.

Programme for the Sunshine Girls' *Jack and the Beanstalk* presented at the Newton Hall, Chapeltown on 12, 13 and 14 March, 1934.

The Sunshine Girls in a production of *All the King's Horses and all the King's Men.* Back row, left to right: Daisy Galloway, Mary North, Audrey Ireran, Betty Schofield, Gwen Birks, Gwen Shaw, Muriel Dawson, Mary Hill. Front: Evelyn Rodgers. This dancing troupe was run in the 1930s by Mrs Wastnedge of Station Road, Chapeltown who spent all her spare time organising the children to put on an annual production in the Newton Hall. Evelyn Rodgers (now Jenkinson) recalls that they were very raw material to work with 'not exactly RADA or Sadlers Wells but it kept us off the streets year after year'. The girls were taken to Jerome's in Sheffield to have their photographs taken in their home-made costumes with a woodland scene backdrop.

A group of regulars from the Midland Hotel (now the Carousel) assembling prior to their charabanc day out.

A coach excursion for the children of Lane End Children's Home organised by Newton Chambers' Business College.

Newton Chambers' staff outing to Edwinstowe, under the Major Oak, *c*. 1900. Back row, left to right: Michael Palmer, Frank Chambers, Ralph Wikely, Jas W. Wikely, J. Faries, Norman Camps, T.S. Hall. Next to back row: H.H. Wood, Scholey Almond, John Hobson, William Foster, William (later Sir William) Jones, William Darwent, R.P. Fisher, William Nesbitt. Next to front row: C.H. Allen, J. Grocutt, H. Ibbotson, F.H. Bewley, Maurice Thompson, William Froggatt. Front row: E. Robinson, P. Coupe, W. Shaw, F. Thompson, C. Spooner and J. Probert.

Newton Chambers' employees posing with David Nixon at Granada TV studios, Manchester in the 1960s.

Dancing round the maypole at Howbrook in the early 1900s.

Dance group at Burncross School, *c.* 1950. The dancers are, left to right, Janet Jubb, Joy Bemrose, Barbara Swift, -?-, Anna Maria Prior.

High Green Amateur Operatic Society in *Maritza* in 1952. Featured are, back row, left to right; Christine Harrison, M. Wilkinson. Front row: Nora Schofield, E. Housley, Alice Weldon and Irene Wilkinson.

Hospital Parade down Thompson Hill, High Green in the 1930s. In the days before the National Health Service was introduced hospitals depended for much of the money they needed on bequests, endowments and public generosity and the parades were started to collect for this good cause. There are many photographs of such parades in the early years of this century. People who lived in a group or row of houses would combine to decorate a cart in secrecy. A metal- or wood-worker would make a frame depicting a particular design which was then covered with coloured paper and other decorative materials. Among the designs remembered are a swan, Ecclesfield church, a coronation carriage and an elephant. The carts had to be ready on the Saturday afternoon of the third weekend after Whitsuntide when judging took place. The parade then set off accompanied by collectors, in the early years of the century, often in fancy dress. The Saturday afternoon parade covered the southern part of the Parish and those with any energy left went to the Feast (fair) beside the Ball Inn in Ecclesfield. On Monday evening the parade re-assembled and proceeded up the hill to Chapeltown, through Burncross to the Crown Inn, turned off to the Rose Inn, down through High Green and Lane End then turned on to Sussex Road and Station Road, ending up at Chapeltown Feast.

The cast of Chapeltown Operatic Society's production of Gilbert and Sullivan's *Yeomen of the Guard* taken in Chapeltown Park. The cast includes Mr Brock, Mr Archer, Clifford Kelsey, Aileen Ellison, Harold Walters, Percy Wikeley and Mrs Wastnedge.

Pit head-gear float for High Green Workers' Day Parade, date unknown, possibly during the Second World War.

Assembling for a parade in connection with the Festival of Britain celebrations at Thorncliffe, July 1951.

Young and old enjoying themselves at the Thorncliffe Festival of Britain celebrations.

'Barrowing', one of the 'Games and Customs of 100 years ago' featured in the Thorncliffe Festival of Britain celebrations. Barrowing was a method used by moulders and miners at Thorncliffe in the past for dealing with an idle colleague. Persistent absenteeism or laziness sometimes resulted in workmates commandeering a wheelbarrow, ropes and blacking bags. They would get the lazy man out of bed early in the morning, make him dress, and truss him up in the barrow. His face would be blacked and then he would be paraded through the district, an object of derision and contempt. He would have been in for a ducking at every pond, trough and brook, and when the party called at a pub he would be left outside, where he might have the beer dregs poured over him. After a final ducking he would be shot out of the barrow and allowed to return home – but only after a promise to work steadily in the future.

Celebrations at Charlton Brook for the Silver Jubilee of King George V and Queen Mary in 1935. These are the residents of 20-28 Stanley Road. Standing, left to right: Mr Whittaker, Amy Prior, Mr J.W. Prior, Edith Prior, Mr Unwin, Kathleen Unwin, Thomas Prior, Mrs Whittaker, Mrs Unwin, Mrs Prior. Kneeling: Grace Prior, Billy Unwin, Violet Whittaker, Phoebe Brook and Charlotte Unwin.

Fancy Dress Parade at Warren to celebrate the coronation of King George VI and Queen Elizabeth, May 1937. Back row, left to right: Olive Smart, Brenda Crookes, Marjorie Andrews, Marjorie Brookes, Dorothy Saxton, Geoffrey Hague, Betty Green, Hilda Newbold, Enid Mellor, Joyce Parkin, ? Crookes and Betty Stutchberry. Front row: Maureen Mellor, Betty Kilner, Maureen Willey (standing in front of BK), Eunice Hill, Jack Smart (sitting on rug), Pat Dransfield, Norman Smith, Donald Eyre, Marion Hague (sitting on rug), Molly Vernon, Mavis Saxton, Joan Sharpe and Edith Bowyer.

The May Queen, her attendants and class mates, Burncross School, 1928.

Coronation tea at Burncross School, 1953.

Mr Durant of Durants' Garage, Chapeltown (see page 33) on a motorcycle of his own make. The number 2 on the front of the bike suggests that he was at some kind of sporting function.

St Andrew's Guild Ramblers from St John's church, Chapeltown in 1936. Back row, left to right: Howard Osbourne (headless), Georges Jacques, Arthur Heathcote, Elsie Huddlestone, Dougie Woods, -?-, Edna Rodgers, Winnie Woods, Percy Moore (behind), Gladys Rodgers and Mabel Shaw. Front row: Ralph Bradbury, Tommy Richardson (leader), Walter Shaw, Arthur Stewart, Will Rawlin and Ronald Pack.

Newton Chambers' Izal Factory workers during their Christmas celebrations. Clarice Hyde, who worked at the factory during the 1960s, recalled that Christmas was a particularly good time, the main thing being the fierce competition to be the best festively decorated room. Each room had a different theme and everything was made out of spare tissue, cardboard and other waste materials. The managers came round and adjudicated; there was no prize, just the prestige.

The queen and her attendants, Parramores' Foundry, Chapeltown. From left to right: Doris Ainsworth, Emily Vaines, Betty Oldknow, Joan French and Kath Croft.

Sisterhood Christmas party at Burncross Chapel.

Dransfield family party, 1956. Horace Dransfield (centre, seated) with Jean Gregory and Philip Ackroyd (grandchildren) on his knee (and Laddie his dog at his feet). Seated on the right are his five sons (the eldest nearest him and the youngest on the far right). Left to right: Eric (with his wife Trissy behind and his son, Peter, kneeling in front), then Cyril (with his wife, Maisie), then Colin (with his wife Nora behind and his son, Stuart in front), then Horace (with his wife, Edna behind and his son, Keith in front) and Jack (with his wife, Dora behind). On the left are his four daughters; Audrey (the eldest and widowed has her three children behind her from left to right, John, Derek and Heather), then Betty (with her husband, Harry Ackroyd behind and Roger her son in front), then Thelma (with her husband Kenneth Gregory behind, her son, Clive is on her knee and her daughter, Joan in front), the youngest daughter is on the left, Irene (with her husband, Wayman Porter behind and her daughter, Catherine in front of her).

Crowds at the coronation celebrations (King George V), 22 June 1911 at Lady's Folly in Tankersley Park (see also page 2). The chimney in the background belongs to Tankersley Colliery.

A reminder that in the days before television and videos families made their own entertainment. Here we see a local cottage interior in the 1930s; the pots have been 'sided', the wireless turned off and a serious game of dominoes is in progress. This photograph was taken by Alan Boulton and on his death his collection became the basis of the Chapeltown and High Green Archive.

Supporters at a Chapeltown and High Green Archive Exhibition and Book Launch, Newton Hall, Chapeltown, June 1994.

Acknowledgements

The authors would like to thank the following for the donation or loan of photographs and/or accompanying information:
Carol Adams, the late Arthur Andrews, Robert Bailey, Charlie Bassender, Ted Bellamy, Terry Bintcliffe, the late Alan Boulton, Gwen Boxford, the late Connie Boyes, Mary Brooks, Freda Casson, Graham Cawthorne, Chris Chapman, Pete Chapman, Barbara Childs, Mary Clarke, Marjorie Copley, David Crisp, John Davis, Bryan Dawson, David Dickinson, Trissy Dransfield, Marjorie Dye, Ken Eastman, Stanley Ellam, the late George Elliott, Jean Ellis, Jim Ellis, Tony Ellis, Mrs Goldingay, Beryl Greaves, Thelma Gregory, Ernest Hartley, the late Wilf Hible, Clara Housley, Jean Huddlestone, Lorna Hulley, Clarice Hyde, Evelyn Jenkinson, Amy Jones, Vicky Kemp, Norman Kirk, Norman Lewis, Carol Limb, Mrs Lister, the late Mrs Maloney, Wilf Marshall, Ivan Martin, Newton Chambers and Co. plc, Margaret Norcliffe, Derek Renshaw, M. Rogalle, the late Gladys Rudkin, Mary Salt, Clifford Shaw, the late George Smith, Winnie Smith, South Riding Estates, J. Staker, Alan Thorne, Jane Thorpe, Maurice Thompson, Mrs Toole, Nora Turp, M. and G. Turton, Jean Varah, Brian Wadsworth, Mrs Watson, A. Wigginton and Freda Woodhead.
The illustration of the spiral staircase is from *The Thorncliffe Records* in Sheffield Archives (TR 75/27). The map of the district was drawn by Bob Warburton.
We apologise if we have inadvertently omitted the name of any contributor.